THE ULTIMATE
Dolphin
BOOK FOR KIDS

JENNY KELLETT

BELLANOVA
MELBOURNE · SOFIA · BERLIN

Copyright © 2023 by Jenny Kellett

Revised 2026.

www.bellanovabooks.com

ISBN: 978-619-264-024-8
Imprint: Bellanova Books

Verify book's Human-Approved Certification at www.authorwing.com/verify

All rights reserved. No part of this book may be reproduced in any form by any electronic or mechanical means including photocopying, recording, or information storage and retrieval without permission in writing from the author.

CONTENTS

Introduction 4
Dolphin Species 6
    Oceanic Dolphins 8
    River Dolphins 12
        Indian River Dolphin 14
        Amazonian River Dolphin 16
        La Plata Dolphin 20
Dolphins vs Porpoises 22
Dolphin Facts 26
Dolphin Conservation 64
Dolphin Quiz 68
    Answers 73
Word search puzzle 74
    Solution 76
Sources 77

INTRODUCTION

It's hard not to love dolphins! But how much do you really know about your favorite marine mammal?

In this book, you will learn over 100 amazing new things about dolphins—from pink Amazon River dolphins to orcas and bottlenose dolphins. You'll be a dolphin expert in no time!

Are you ready? *Let's go!*

DOLPHIN SPECIES

Dolphins come in all shapes and sizes. In fact, there are over 35 different species, which can be divided into oceanic dolphins and river dolphins.

There are four living families of dolphins, in which these different species live:
- *Delphinidae* (oceanic dolphins),
- *Platanistidae* (Indian river dolphins),
- *Iniidae* (New World river dolphins),
- *Pontoporiidae* (La Plata dolphin).

Let's take a closer look at the differences!

OCEANIC DOLPHINS

Oceanic dolphins are a diverse group of dolphins that live in open oceans and deep seas. They are highly social animals and often travel in groups, known as **pods**.

Some common species of oceanic dolphins include the **short-finned pilot whale, the spinner dolphin, bottlenose dolphins,** and **the common dolphin**.

Oceanic dolphins vary greatly in size. The smallest dolphin in this family is the Maui's dolphin, measuring 1.7 m (5 ft 7 in) in length and weighing 50 kg (110 lbs).

Four orcas seen in California.

The largest known dolphin, the orca, which can grow up to 9.4 m (31 ft) and weigh as much as 10 metric tons (11 short tons), also belongs to the oceanic dolphin family.

Spinner dolphins seen in Hawaii.

Oceanic dolphins have a streamlined body shape, allowing them to swim at high speeds and easily maneuver through the water. They are also excellent divers and can hold their breath for several minutes at a time.

Although oceanic dolphins can be found across most of the world, most species prefer to live in warmer waters around the tropics. However, some, like the right whale dolphin, prefer colder climates.

Oceanic dolphins are known for their intelligence and playful behavior, which often includes jumping and breaching the surface of the water.

RIVER DOLPHINS

River dolphins are found in freshwater rivers and deltas in Asia, South America, and some parts of Africa. They are different from their ocean cousins in many ways, including their physical appearance and behaviors.

There are three different living families of river dolphins. Sadly, a fourth family of river dolphins, the Yangtze river dolphin (*Lipotidae*), is believed to have recently become extinct.

Let's take a closer look at the different living families.

Amazon river dolphin.

© Jorge Andrade

INDIAN RIVER DOLPHINS

Indian river dolphins are a species of river dolphins found in the rivers of the Indian subcontinent. This family has two dolphins: the **Ganges river dolphin** and the **Indus river dolphin**. It's easy to recognize these dolphins by their long, thin beaks and stocky bodies. They also have special adaptations for freshwater, including seeing well in murky water.

The Indian river dolphin often lives in pods of up to 10 individuals. They are an important part of the river ecosystem and play a crucial role in maintaining the food chain balance.

A Ganges river dolphin. © Gregoire Dubois

Unfortunately, Indian river dolphins face many threats, including habitat loss and fragmentation due to the construction of dams and other human activities. Water pollution and the use of nets and other fishing gear also threaten these dolphins.

AMAZONIAN RIVER DOLPHINS

The **Iniidae** family of dolphins includes two species of freshwater dolphins that are found in South America: the **Amazon river dolphin** and the **Tucuxi dolphin**.

River dolphins belong to several families. The Amazon river dolphin (boto) is in the family Iniidae. The tucuxi, although it lives in rivers and estuaries, is more closely related to marine dolphins (family *Delphinidae*).

Amazon river dolphins. © Kevin Schafer

The Amazon river dolphin, also known as the boto, is the largest species of freshwater dolphin. It is found in the Amazon Basin and is well adapted to life in the murky, slow-moving waters of the river.

The boto has a long, narrow snout and a flexible neck, which allows it to maneuver easily in tight spaces and catch prey. It is also known for its pink color, which is caused by blood vessels near the surface of its skin.

The Tucuxi dolphin is a smaller species that is found in the coastal waters and estuaries of South America. It has a more streamlined body than the boto and is more closely related to marine dolphins.

Both species of *Iniidae* dolphins are highly social and are often seen in pods. Unfortunately, both species are considered to be threatened due to human activities such as habitat destruction, pollution, and accidental capture in fishing nets.

Expédition de F. de Castelnau (Amérique du Sud). 7ᵉ Partie. Zoologie. Mammifères. Pl. 19.

Early drawings of river dolphins. The first two are Tucuxi dolphins, the third an Amazon River dolphin.

1. DELPHINUS PALLIDUS.   2. DELPHINUS FLUVIATILIS.
3. INIA GEOFFRENSIS.

LA PLATA DOLPHIN

The **Pontoporiidae** family includes only one species of dolphin, the La Plata dolphin, also known as the Franciscana. This species is found along the coasts of South America, particularly in the estuaries of the Rio de la Plata in Argentina and Uruguay.

The La Plata dolphin is a small species, with adults typically reaching lengths of about 1.5 m (4.9 ft) and weights of around 50 kg (110 lbs).

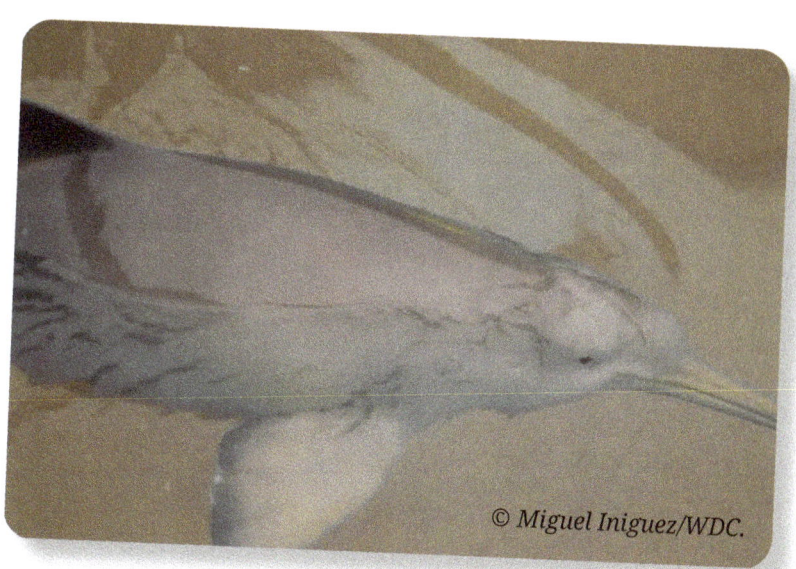

© Miguel Iniguez/WDC.

It has a distinctive appearance, with a narrow snout and a long, thin beak. The La Plata dolphin has a dark grey to brown dorsal side and a lighter belly, and it is sometimes referred to as the "skunk dolphin" because of the light grey stripe that runs from its eye to its flippers.

Unfortunately, the La Plata dolphin is considered to be endangered.

DOLPHINS VS PORPOISES

Dolphins and porpoises are both members of the cetacean family, which also includes whales. However, they are different species and have some distinct physical and behavioral characteristics.

One of the main differences between dolphins and porpoises is their physical appearance. Dolphins tend to have a more curved dorsal fin, while porpoises have a more triangular dorsal fin. Also, dolphins usually have a longer snout, while porpoises have a more rounded snout.

Yangtze finless porpoises.

Another difference is their teeth. Porpoises have spade-shaped teeth, while dolphins have cone-shaped teeth.

An oceanic dolphin in Eilat, Israel.

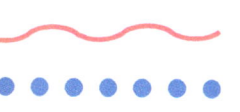

Dolphins are generally larger and more sociable than porpoises, and they are known for their acrobatic displays and playful behavior. Porpoises, on the other hand, tend to be more solitary and less vocal than dolphins.

Also, dolphins are found in all the oceans and some rivers, while porpoises are mostly found in cold waters of the North Pacific and North Atlantic, and the Arctic.

In general, porpoises are less studied than dolphins and less commonly kept in captivity, which means that we know less about their behavior and biology.

DOLPHIN FACTS

Dolphins have to choose to breathe every single time. They don't breathe automatically like humans do, so even when they're resting, they still have to remember to come up for air.

• • •

Dolphins can sleep with half their brain at a time. One side rests while the other side stays awake enough to keep swimming, watch for danger, and make sure they don't forget to breathe.

Sometimes a resting dolphin will float so still at the surface that it looks like a piece of driftwood. Scientists even have a name for this: "logging."

• • •

Most dolphin babies are born tail-first, which is a smart safety trick. That way, the baby stays underwater until the very last moment and doesn't accidentally inhale water.

• • •

Right after a dolphin calf is born, its mom helps it reach the surface for its first breath. She may gently push or guide the baby upward so it can take its very first gulp of air.

• • •

Dolphins can "see" underwater using sound, even when it's dark or cloudy. They make clicking noises, listen for the echoes, and build a sound-picture in their minds—this is called **echolocation**.

A dolphin's lower jaw helps it hear underwater in a surprising way. The jaw is filled with special fatty tissue that carries sound toward the ears, almost like a built-in sound receiver.

• • •

Dolphins can hear extremely high-pitched sounds that humans can't detect. Their hearing is so sensitive that tiny squeaks and clicks can be useful information instead of just noise.

Dolphins use different sounds for different jobs. Clicks are great for hunting and exploring, while whistles are used more for communication and social life.

• • •

Many dolphins create their own special whistle that works like a name. This "signature whistle" helps other dolphins recognize them in a noisy ocean.

• • •

Echolocation can be unbelievably precise. Some studies suggest dolphins can tell the difference between objects even when they're hidden inside something, like a container.

• • •

Some scientists think dolphins may be able to sense Earth's magnetic field like a built-in compass. It's a fascinating idea, but researchers are still working to prove exactly how it works.

THE ULTIMATE DOLPHIN BOOK

Dolphins can remember each other for a very long time. In studies, dolphins recognized familiar whistles even after being apart for more than 20 years.

• • •

Dolphins have large, powerful brains built for social life. They are especially good at teamwork, problem-solving, and understanding what other dolphins might be thinking or feeling.

• • •

Dolphin brains contain rare "social" brain cells that are also found in humans and great apes. These special neurons may help with bonding, cooperation, and complex relationships.

• • •

Some dolphin families pass down clever skills like traditions. A young dolphin can learn special hunting tricks by watching its mother and copying what she does.

A Hector dolphin in New Zealand.

In parts of Australia, some dolphins protect their noses while hunting by using sea sponges like tools. They wear the sponge on their snout so sharp rocks don't scrape them as they search the seafloor.

• • •

In a few places, dolphins and humans have worked together to catch fish. Dolphins may signal fishers when to throw their nets, and both the people and dolphins end up with a better meal.

• • •

Dolphins can copy sounds and movements on purpose. They can imitate other dolphins—and sometimes even mimic human actions or noises.

• • •

Most dolphins live in social groups called pods, and they often travel together. Staying in a pod helps them find food, avoid danger, and raise babies more safely.

When food is everywhere, dolphin groups can join together into giant gatherings called **superpods**. These huge meet-ups can include hundreds or even thousands of dolphins.

· · ·

In some species, male dolphins form long-lasting friendships and alliances. These partnerships can last for years and help them protect each other or compete against rivals.

· · ·

Dolphin calves aren't raised by their mothers alone. Other adults in the pod may help babysit, protect the baby, and keep it safe while the mother hunts.

A pod of wild orcas in Norway.   >

A pod of dolphins in the Bahamas.

Dolphin milk is extremely rich and fatty, which helps calves grow quickly and stay warm in the water. A calf needs lots of energy because it's swimming almost from day one.

• • •

Newborn dolphin calves can look a little wrinkly at first. They're born with temporary "fetal folds," which are small creases that fade after a few days.

• • •

Orcas are actually the largest type of dolphin, and they often live in family groups led by older females. These "grandma" orcas can help the whole group survive by guiding and protecting younger members.

• • •

Dolphins don't only communicate with sound—they also communicate through touch. Gentle rubbing, flipper pats, and body contact can help dolphins bond and stay friendly.

Dolphins don't chew their food like humans do. They use their teeth to grab slippery prey, then swallow it whole.

• • •

A dolphin's stomach works in two main sections. One part can hold food quickly, while the other part breaks it down later, which is helpful when meals need to be eaten fast.

• • •

Dolphins can smack the water with their tails so hard that it stuns fish. A quick tail slap can turn a fast-moving fish into an easy snack.

• • •

Some dolphins hunt as a team by herding fish into a tight, swirling clump called a bait ball. Once the fish are packed together, dolphins take turns rushing in to eat.

An Indo-Pacific bottlenose dolphin.

Amazon river dolphins.

A few dolphins use a risky hunting trick called shore-stranding. They slide onto the beach to grab fish near the shore, then wiggle and flop their way back into the water.

• • •

Even within the same dolphin species, diets can change depending on where they live. Dolphins in one area might eat mostly fish, while dolphins elsewhere might hunt squid or other prey.

• • •

In dark or murky water, echolocation becomes a dolphin's most important hunting tool. When eyes aren't enough, sound helps them find prey they can't see.

• • •

Some dolphins share food with others in their pod. Passing prey around may strengthen friendships, help younger dolphins learn, or keep the group working together.

Dolphins can reach speeds of about 18–20 miles per hour (30 km/h) in short bursts. That's fast enough to make them look like underwater rockets!

• • •

Every dolphin fin has a job. Flippers help steer, the dorsal fin helps balance, and the tail flukes provide the powerful push that drives them forward.

• • •

Dolphins move their tails up and down when they swim. Fish usually wag side to side, so dolphin swimming looks different because their whole body flexes vertically.

• • •

Jumping out of the water can actually help dolphins travel faster. At high speed, leaping reduces drag, which can save energy during long swims.

Dolphins in South Africa.

Dolphins often "porpoise," meaning they skim in and out of the water while swimming quickly. This pattern helps them move fast without getting as tired.

• • •

Dolphin skin stays smooth because it renews quickly. A slick body creates less resistance in the water, which helps dolphins swim efficiently.

• • •

River dolphins are built for twisting, turning waterways instead of open-ocean speed. They're often slower, but they're amazing at sharp turns in tight spaces.

• • •

Dolphins can store extra oxygen in their bodies for diving. Their blood and muscles hold lots of oxygen so they can stay underwater longer without needing to breathe.

When dolphins dive, their heart rate can slow down to save oxygen. Their bodies also send more blood to the most important organs, like the brain and heart.

• • •

Dolphin lungs can partially collapse during deep dives, which helps protect them from pressure changes. This is one reason they can dive without getting "the bends" like human scuba divers.

• • •

Dolphins can heal from injuries surprisingly well, but they aren't invincible. Deep wounds can still get infected, especially in polluted water.

• • •

Dolphins don't grow new teeth as they age. Since they keep the same teeth for life, older dolphins may struggle more if their teeth wear down or break.

Dolphins produce tears to protect their eyes. Tears help clean the surface of the eye and keep it healthy.

• • •

Dolphins can see well in dim underwater light. Their eyes have lots of rod cells, which are special cells that help animals see in low-light conditions.

• • •

Most dolphins probably don't see bright colors the way humans do. Many scientists think dolphins see mostly shades of gray or limited color.

• • •

Dolphins can be hunted by large predators like sharks and orcas. Even smart, fast animals aren't always the top hunters in the ocean.

Fishing nets can be deadly for dolphins because thin lines are hard to detect. Dolphins may get trapped by accident, which is called bycatch.

The ocean is getting noisier, and that can confuse dolphins. Loud boat engines and sonar can make it harder for them to communicate, hunt, and find their way.

Some pollution doesn't disappear—it builds up inside animals over time. Harmful chemicals can collect in dolphin blubber and may affect their health and their babies.

Dolphins can be hit by boats in busy waterways. Fast-moving boats and crowded areas can turn feeding and traveling into a dangerous challenge.

A Chilean dolphin. © *Francisco Castro Carmona*

A pan-tropical spotted dolphin.

River dolphins are some of the most endangered dolphins in the world. Dams, pollution, and heavy boat traffic can make rivers difficult and unsafe places to live.

• • •

Protected ocean areas can give dolphins a better chance to survive. When fishing, boat traffic, or noise is limited, dolphins and their prey often recover more easily.

• • •

Watching dolphins in the wild should be done with respect. If people chase, crowd, or feed dolphins, it can stress them out and change their natural behavior.

• • •

Climate change can shift where fish and squid live. When prey moves to new waters, dolphins may have to change their routes and hunting habits too.

THE ULTIMATE DOLPHIN BOOK

Scientists use many tools to protect dolphins better. Photo ID, genetics, sound recordings, and satellite tags help researchers learn where dolphins go and what they need.

• • •

Millions of years ago, the ancestors of dolphins lived on land and had legs. Over time, they returned to the ocean and slowly evolved into the sleek swimmers we know today.

Baby dolphins can't latch onto a nipple the way human babies do. Instead, the mother squirts milk straight into the calf's mouth so it can drink underwater without swallowing seawater.

• • •

Amazon river dolphins can turn their heads more than most ocean dolphins. Their neck bones aren't fused, which helps them twist and hunt in narrow, tangled river spaces.

• • •

In parts of Florida, bottlenose dolphins use an amazing hunting trick called mud-ring fishing. They swirl in a circle to kick up a muddy ring, trapping fish inside until the fish panic and jump right into their mouths.

• • •

Dolphins sometimes surf the waves made by boats. Riding the bow wave can be fun, and it can also give them a free boost forward without extra effort.

A dolphin may pop its head out of the water to look around, which is called a **spyhop**. It's like using their head as a periscope to check what's happening above the surface.

• • •

A loud tail slap on the surface can send a clear message. Dolphins may use it to warn others, show excitement, or even startle fish during a hunt.

• • •

Every dolphin dorsal fin has a unique shape with tiny nicks and notches. Scientists use fin photos like fingerprints to recognize individual dolphins over time.

• • •

Researchers can even collect dolphin "snot" to check their health. Special drones fly through the misty blow from a dolphin's blowhole and gather tiny samples for testing.

A bottlenose dolphin.

Dolphins can keep their bodies warm using a clever heat-saving system. Special blood vessels in their fins and flippers help control heat loss so they don't get too cold.

• • •

Dolphin eyes are built for both bright sunlight and deep water darkness. Their pupils can change shape, and they can even move each eye separately to watch two different things at once.

• • •

Orcas come in different "types," and not all of them eat the same food. Some orca groups mostly eat fish, while others hunt marine mammals, and each group can have its own dialect of sounds.

• • •

Different dolphin species can have very different numbers of teeth. Some have more than 100, while others, like Risso's dolphins, have far fewer teeth that can wear down quickly.

Risso's dolphins often look like they've been scratched all over, and there's a reason for that. They fight with squid, and the squid's beaks and tentacles can leave pale scars on their skin.

• • •

Young dolphins practice making sounds the way human babies practice talking. Calves often "babble" with clicks and whistles before they learn the exact sounds adults use.

• • •

When a shark shows up, dolphins may work together to defend themselves. Some pods have been seen surrounding a shark and charging at it to drive it away.

Abandoned fishing nets called ghost nets can keep trapping animals for years. Dolphins can get tangled in them long after the nets were lost or thrown away.

• • •

In places with glowing plankton, dolphins can look magical at night. As they swim, they may leave bright blue-green trails that sparkle in the water.

• • •

Sometimes entire groups of dolphins strand on beaches at the same time. This can happen if the pod follows a sick or confused leader, and rescuers try to keep the dolphins wet, cool, and supported until they can be guided back out.

DOLPHIN
CONSERVATION

Dolphins are beautiful creatures, but unfortunately, many dolphin species face threats due to human activities such as pollution, overfishing, and accidental capture in fishing lines.

Climate change and habitat destruction also affect the lives of many species.

Maui's dolphin, the Ganges River dolphin, and the Indus dolphin are some of the most endangered dolphin species.

Fortunately, many people care a lot about dolphins and work hard to protect their futures. Some of the organizations that work with dolphins include *Whale and Dolphin Conservation*, *Dolphin Project,* and the *WWF.*

But you don't need to be a scientist to help dolphins. There are lots of ways you can help protect their habitats wherever you live. Preventing pollution, reducing the amount of plastics we use, and recycling will all help protect the oceans and rivers where dolphins live.

How can YOU help?

Here are a few more ways that you can help dolphins:

- **Learn about dolphins and their habitats.** Educate yourself about the different species of dolphins and the threats they face. Share what you learn with your friends and family.
- **Reduce plastic use.** Plastic pollution is a major threat to dolphins and other marine life. Encourage your family to use reusable bags, water bottles, and containers, and to properly dispose of trash.

- **Support conservation organizations.** You can support organizations that work to protect dolphins and their habitats.
- **Spread the word.** Ask your family and friends for donations to your favorite dolphin organization instead of gifts on your birthday and holidays.
- **Beach clean-ups.** If you live near the ocean, you can participate in beach clean-up events in your community to help keep our oceans clean.
- **Support sustainable fishing.** Look for labels on fish products to make sure that they are dolphin-friendly.
- **Get involved in local conservation efforts.** Ask your school or community if they have any conservation projects or volunteer opportunities that you can get involved in.

DOLPHIN *Quiz*

Now test your knowledge in our dolphin quiz! Answers are on page 73.

1. Why are fishing lines so dangerous for dolphins?

2. What do dolphins use to "see" with sound?

3. Dolphins lay eggs. True or false?

4. Are dolphins warm-blooded or cold-blooded?

5 What is a male dolphin called?

6 What is the tail of a dolphin called?

7 How many stomachs does a dolphin have?

8 What is the smallest species of dolphin?

9 How many families of living river dolphins are there?

10 What is a baby dolphin called?

11 What color is the Chilean dolphin?

12 What is a dolphin's thick layer of fat called?

13 How much does the average dolphin weigh at birth?

14 How often do dolphins breathe?

15 On average, how long do dolphins live for?

16 Which species of dolphin is pink?

17 What is a group of dolphins called?

18 What is the largest species of dolphin?

19 How many species of dolphins are there?

20 Where do La Plata dolphins live?

ANSWERS

1. Dolphins' sonar can't detect them, so they get trapped in them.
2. Echolocation.
3. False.
4. Warm-blooded.
5. A bull.
6. The fluke.
7. Two.
8. Maui's dolphin.
9. Three.
10. A calf.
11. Black.
12. Blubber.
13. Around 30 kg (66 lbs).
14. Every 2-3 minutes.
15. 25 years.
16. Amazon river dolphin.
17. A pod.
18. Orca.
19. Around 37.
20. The coast of South America.

Dolphins
WORD SEARCH

```
F  B  O  T  T  L  E  N  O  S  E  T
D  T  D  O  L  P  H  I  N  K  X  O
S  R  P  O  R  T  Y  U  I  I  V  C
A  E  D  S  R  C  B  D  S  L  C  E
X  S  G  F  D  S  A  S  D  L  F  A
C  M  Q  Y  Z  C  A  L  F  E  M  N
J  F  A  X  C  V  H  L  K  R  D  S
H  D  H  R  D  S  A  D  F  W  H  G
G  S  A  S  I  D  F  A  S  H  S  D
A  M  A  Z  O  N  G  F  D  A  C  Z
D  N  B  V  X  Z  E  E  R  L  C  X
S  F  P  O  R  P  O  I  S  E  A  D
```

Can you find all the words below in the word search puzzle on the left?

DOLPHIN   OCEAN   BOTTLENOSE

DORSAL   CALF   KILLER WHALE

AMAZON   MARINE   PORPOISE

THE ULTIMATE DOLPHIN BOOK

SOLUTION

	B	O	T	T	L	E	N	O	S	E	
		D	O	L	P	H	I	N	K		O
			O					I			C
				R				L			E
					S			L			A
	M				C	A	L	F	E		N
		A				L		R			
		R						W			
		I						H			
A	M	A	Z	O	N			A			
					E			L			
	P	O	R	P	O	I	S	E			

SOURCES

"Dolphin Facts And Information - Whale And Dolphin Conservation". 2023. Whale & Dolphin Conservation UK. https://uk.whales.org/whales-dolphins/facts-about-dolphins.

"Facts - Adopt A Dolphin". 2023. Adopt A Dolphin. https://www.adoptadolphin.org.uk/facts.

"Dolphin | Facts & Pictures". 2023. Encyclopedia Britannica. https://www.britannica.com/animal/dolphin-mammal.

"River Dolphin - Wikipedia". 2023. En.Wikipedia.Org. https://en.wikipedia.org/wiki/River_dolphin.

"Freshwater Dolphin Species And Facts". 2023. World Wildlife Fund. https://www.worldwildlife.org/stories/freshwater-dolphin-species-and-facts.

"Ganges River Dolphin | Freshwater Dolphin | Species | WWF". 2023. World Wildlife Fund. https://www.worldwildlife.org/species/ganges-river-dolhin.

"Amazon River Dolphin - Wikipedia". 2023. En.Wikipedia.Org. https://en.wikipedia.org/wiki/Amazon_river_dolphin.

"Whales &Amp; Coastal Dolphins - WCS.Org". 2023. Wcs.Org. https://www.wcs.org/our-work/wildlife/whales-coastal-dolphins.

"Facts About Hector's And Māui Dolphin". 2023. Doc.Govt.Nz. https://www.doc.govt.nz/nature/native-animals/marine-mammals/dolphins/maui-dolphin/facts/. "How Many Species Of Dolphins Are There?". 2023. Whale & Dolphin Conservation UK. https://uk.whales.org/whales-dolphins/how-many-species-of-dolphins-are-there/.

"9 Mind-Boggling Dolphin Facts". 2023. Treehugger. https://www.treehugger.com/mind-boggling-dolphin-facts-4863589.

"Common Bottlenose Dolphin - Wikipedia". 2023. En.Wikipedia.Org. https://en.wikipedia.org/wiki/Common_bottlenose_dolphin.

Did you love learning about dolphins?!
We'd love it if you left us a **review**—
they always make us smile, but more
importantly they help other readers make
better buying decisions.

Thanks for your support!

Visit us at

www.bellanovabooks.com

**for more fun fact books
and giveaways!**

ALSO BY JENNY KELLETT

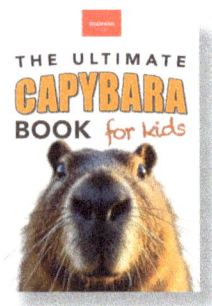  

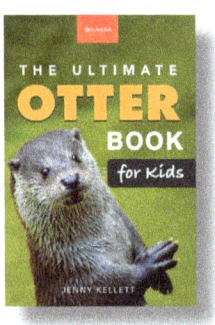  

... and more!

Available at

www.bellanovabooks.com

and all major online bookstores.